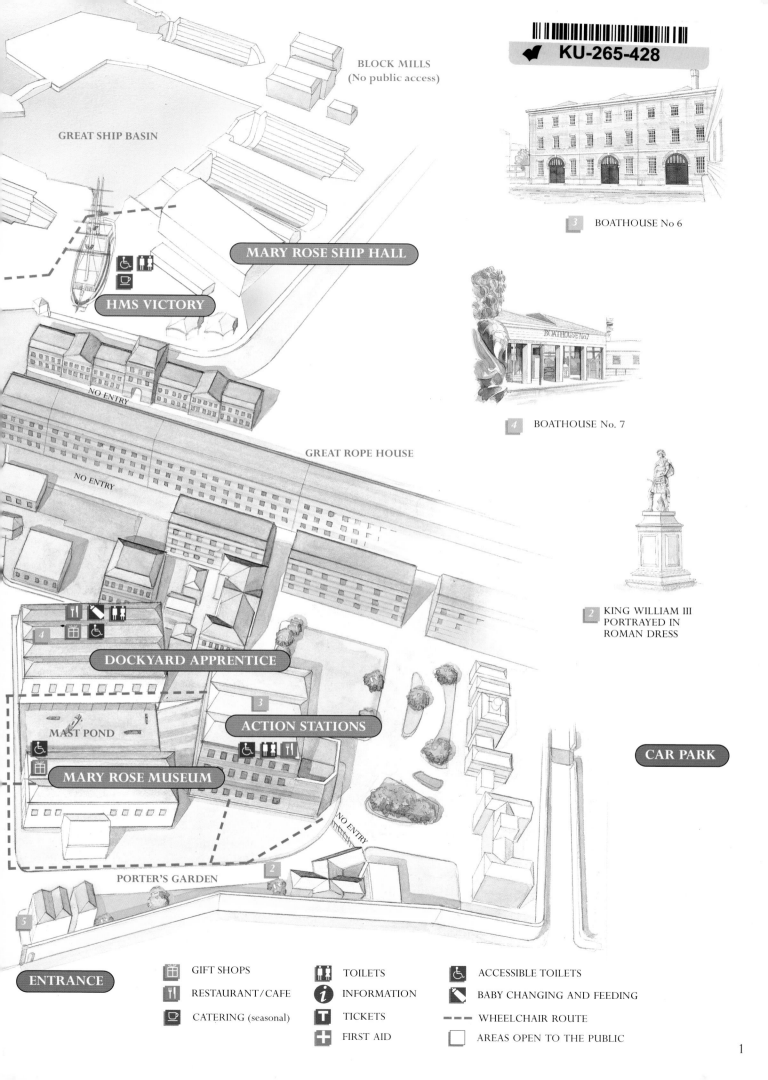

BLOCK MILLS
(No public access)

GREAT SHIP BASIN

BOATHOUSE No 6

MARY ROSE SHIP HALL

HMS VICTORY

BOATHOUSE No. 7

NO ENTRY

GREAT ROPE HOUSE

NO ENTRY

KING WILLIAM III
PORTRAYED IN
ROMAN DRESS

DOCKYARD APPRENTICE

ACTION STATIONS

CAR PARK

MAST POND

MARY ROSE MUSEUM

NO ENTRY

PORTER'S GARDEN

ENTRANCE

	GIFT SHOPS		TOILETS		ACCESSIBLE TOILETS
	RESTAURANT/CAFE		INFORMATION		BABY CHANGING AND FEEDING
	CATERING (seasonal)		TICKETS	- - -	WHEELCHAIR ROUTE
			FIRST AID		AREAS OPEN TO THE PUBLIC

1

CONTENTS

PORTSMOUTH HISTORIC DOCKYARD

Surrounded by the modern Royal Navy at work, Portsmouth Historic Dockyard embraces three of the greatest warships ever built, *Mary Rose*, HMS *Victory*, and HMS *Warrior* 1860.
These magnificent ships, in combination with the historic buildings and docks, embody Britain's naval history, threaded together by the Royal Naval Museum, and captures today's Navy with ACTION STATIONS.

THE GUIDE

There are four colour-coded sections, each covering a period of naval history. Each section tells the history of the Navy and of the Dockyard over that period, and describes the attraction at Portsmouth Historic Dockyard which represents the era.

WANT TO KNOW MORE?

Some attractions have a fully illustrated guide book of their own. They can be bought in any of the shops in the Historic Dockyard.

THE RISE OF T

The sea has always played a major role in Britain's history. The waters of the Solent and Portsmouth Harbour have been crucial to defence since the Romans established a force in the Channel, under the Count of the Saxon Shore, based at Portchester at the head of the harbour. Later, King Alfred, according to legend, commanded a fleet which repelled Viking invaders off the Isle of Wight in 897.

Early ships were small and seldom ventured beyond coastal waters. Usually, they were dual-purpose: merchant-men in peacetime, converting to warships in wartime.

Battles were fought at very close quarters, with men fighting hand-to-hand duels.

Improvements in design and ship building methods in the medieval period produced larger, ocean-going vessels. They ventured further afield and the first voyages of exploration began. Relics of the period before 1500 are few, but the Royal Naval Museum houses some planks from *Grace Dieu*, the flagship of Henry V.

Guns were first taken to sea in the 1400s, leading to the development of purpose-built warships. One of the first of these was the famous *Mary Rose*,

the 'flower' of Henry VIII's fine war-fleet. From those early warships evolved the fast, powerful, Elizabethan galleons which helped to defeat the Spanish Armada in 1588. Tactics, however, remained relatively primitive and the organisation - especially for the provision of pay and supplies - haphazard.

During the 17th century, a more organised approach to the provision of a regular war-fleet developed. Ships became standardised: heavily gunned line-of-battleships which did the actual fighting; lighter, faster craft for scouting. Battle tactics became more

The defeat of the Spanish Armada 1588 by W. L. Wyllie

	1200	1300	1400	1450
Society & Technology	Gunpowder introduced to Europe Gothic cathedrals Marco Polo	Black Death First English Bible Dante Chaucer	Golf played in Scotland	Da Gama, Columbus, Cabot reach Ind West Indies, North America
War & Politics	Magna Carta 5th Crusade	———Hundred Years War Crecy	—Joan of Arc Agincourt	Wars of the Roses Henry Tudor (VII)
Navy	Portsmouth squadron protects south coast	First fleet battle at Sluys First fleet review - by Henry V at Portsmouth		
Portsmouth	First dock Burnt by Dover pirates Dock wall built	Burnt by French	Round Tower defends harbour entrance -first artillery coastal defence	World's first dry dock

HE ROYAL NAVY

formal and pre-planned. Officers, who had previously moved between land and sea, became maritime specialists. In 1664, the Navy gained its own seagoing soldiers, the Duke of York's Maritime Regiment of Foot, forerunner of the Royal Marines - a private of the regiment is shown here.

At the same time, under gifted officials such as Samuel Pepys, the administration of the Navy was centralised and a system of supply and operational control was established. A network of naval dockyards was created in southern England, Portsmouth taking pride of place.

Throughout this century, England's main opponent was the Dutch Republic. Three bloody wars were fought over control of the Channel and overseas trade. Peace only came when William of Orange became King of England as the consort of Queen Mary, following the Glorious Revolution of 1688.

By 1700, the phrase 'the Royal Navy' was in general use. It was a standing force with fine ships, a permanent corps of professional officers, an efficient supporting civil service and a distinguished battle record. With the Dutch now allies, the stage was set for a long series of wars with France.

The Dutch Wars: The Battle of North Foreland 1653 by W. L. Wyllie as seen in the Royal Naval Museum's Sailing Navy Gallery

1500	1550	1600	1650	
High Renaissance Reformation	Magellan	Counter Reformation	Shakespeare	Pilgrim Fathers	Great Fire of London	Christopher Wren
		Baroque Art		*Vasa* sinks in Stockholm	First paper money
Henry VIII	Dissolution of monastries	Elizabeth I	East India Company	English Civil War	Restoration of Charles II
Field of the Cloth of Gold		French retake Calais	Gunpowder Plot	Louis XIV	Charles I beheaded	Glorious Revolution
Mary Rose	Navy Board established		Spanish Armada		Dutch Wars	Pepys	Captain Kidd
French Wars		Drake's circumnavigation	James I's cutbacks	Marines created	hanged for piracy
First chain across harbour	Fire devastation		Departure to Virginia of first American colonists	Falls to Parliament after siege	
First ship built - *Sweepstake*					Mast pond excavated

We order you, without delay, by the view of
lawful men, to cause our docks at
Portsmouth to be enclosed with a
Good & Strong wall …for the preservation of
our Ships and Galleys
By order of King John 20th May 1212

THE EARLY DAYS OF THE DOCKYARD

As the best natural shelter on the south coast, Portsmouth Harbour was the key to defence and trade for Britons, Romans, Saxons and Normans in succession.

Like the Romans, the Normans controlled the harbour from the northern end at Portchester. They built a new castle in the remains of the Roman fort. They used Portsea Island, at the entrance to the harbour, as a gathering place for their armies on their way to and from the other half of the kingdom in France. Storehouses and workshops sprang up to provision and maintain the King's ships and, in 1194, Richard I granted the town, called Portsmouth, its first charter and ordered a dock to be built. In 1212, King John ordered the Sheriff of Southampton to build a wall around the new dockyard.

The event which most clearly marks Portsmouth Dockyard's rise to national prominence was the construction of the world's first dry dock in 1495, an innovation prompted by the advent of large warships. In 1510, the keel of the *Mary Rose* was laid in the Dockyard and, two years later, Portsmouth was officially appointed a building centre for the King's ships.

No traces of the medieval dockyard remain. The original dry dock lies under the Great Ship Basin, near HMS *Victory*, and the wooden buildings have long been replaced.

THE WORLD'S FIRST DRY DOCK

In the middle ages, when the hull of a ship had to be repaired, it was simply laid on its side as the tide went out. This was not particularly satisfactory because it only allowed a few working hours until the tide came back in, and it was not good for the ship. As warships got larger, a better solution was needed.

King Henry VII entrusted the problem to Sir Reginald Bray, the architect of magnificent new chapels at Westminster Abbey and Windsor Castle. His radical new dock was 61m (200ft long), 20 m (65 ft) wide and 9m (30ft) deep. Its sides were built of wood, reinforced with stone. Once the ship had been floated in, the entrance was blocked by a pair of gates, each extending across the full width. The gap between the gates was filled with clay and shingle to make them watertight. An 'Ingyn' - probably a horse-powered bucket and chain pump - was used to remove the water from the dock. As the water was removed, wooden props were placed between the ship's sides and the dock wall to keep it upright - the same principle as used today.

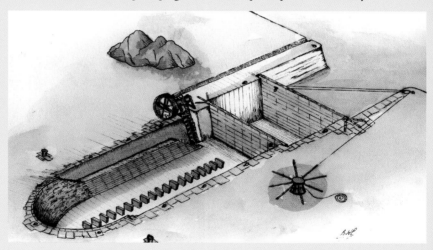

In May 1496, the *Sovereigne* was the first ship to enter the new dock. The operation required 280 men working 24 hours. Getting it out again, after an eight month refit, was just as difficult. Twenty men took four days to remove the clay and shingle from between the dock gates before they could be opened.

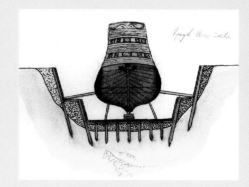

1 The upper deck and castle decks were fighting areas, and when the *Mary Rose* sank they were packed with gunners, soldiers, archers and all their equipment. Large iron and bronze guns were ready to bombard the opposing French ships, and pikes, bills, and handguns were at hand for close fighting. Removable blinds on the upper deck provided ports for the archers.

2 The heaviest guns, with all their associated equipment, were stationed along the main deck. Ventilation hatches let the smoke and fumes escape.

Three almost intact cabins were found on the main deck. These belonged to the pilot **3** the barber-surgeon **4** and the carpenters **5** and contained the tools of their professions. The tools shown below were amongst the many items recovered from the carpenters' cabin and include their mallets, braces, augers, moulding planes and whetstones. Poignantly, the remains of a dog were found trapped in the sliding door of this cabin.

6 Excavation of the orlop deck uncovered stores and equipment: coils of rope, rigging blocks, spare parts for the gun carriages, chests and barrels - some of which contained provisions including beef, fish and fruit.

MARY ROSE
'The Flower of all Ships'

7 The hold contained ballast, stores, victualling equipment and the ship's galley, consisting of two large cauldrons over a brick-built firebox. Large quantities of logs for the fire were found nearby. The pump took water from the bottom of the ship to the upper deck, where it flowed overboard in a waterway called a 'dale'.

FACTS AND FIGURES

As the ship was:

Length at waterline	38.5m (126ft 4in)
Total length	45m (147ft 8in)
Beam	11.66m (38ft 3in)
Draught	4.6m (15ft 1in)
Height at stern	14m (45ft 11in)
Displacement	c 715 tonnes (700 tons)
Crew	415 (200 mariners, 30 gunners, 185 soldiers)

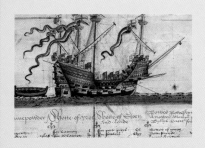

A Distinguished Career

1509-1511
Built at Portsmouth on the orders of the newly crowned King Henry VIII

1512-1514
Flagship of the King's fleet for his first French war

1522
Flagship for second French war

1536
Major refit

19 July 1545
Capsizes in the Solent during skirmish with French fleet

1545-1546
Unsuccessful salvage attempts

1836
Pioneering divers, John and Charles Deane, rediscover the site and raise items including guns

1965
Alexander McKee starts search for the ship

1971
Divers see first exposed timbers

1978-1982
Contents recovered in world's largest underwater excavation, led by Margaret Rule

11 October 1982
Hull raised and towed into Portsmouth

30 September 1994
Start of spraying with water-soluble wax to conserve the hull

October 2005
Latest dives recover the massive stem timber and anchor from the wreck site

A PIONEERING WARSHIP

The *Mary Rose* was one of the earliest warships built to carry heavy guns. As no detailed models, drawings or records of ships from this period have survived, she gives a unique insight into Tudor shipbuilding techniques.

The challenge faced by Henry VIII's shipwrights was to get more and bigger guns on to the ship without making it unstable. To do this, they needed to place guns nearer the waterline. The gun ports there had to be watertight in rough seas, but this was difficult with traditional 'clinker-built' construction which overlaps the planks on the outside of the hull, creating an uneven surface.

The newly introduced edge-to-edge carvel planking of the *Mary Rose* gave a smooth finish to the lower hull which allowed gun ports, with lids that could be sealed, to be inserted.

When the ship was excavated, divers discovered the heavy guns run out through these ports. Failure to close the gun ports and prevent water coming through them is probably one reason the ship sank. A survivor reported that when the *Mary Rose* heeled over with the wind, the water entered by the lowest row of gun ports, which had been left open after firing.

The hull was mainly built of oak, although part of the keel and the orlop deck planks were made of elm, and other woods were used for specific purposes. It is mostly fastened together using oak treenails (pegs), with some iron bolts for additional security. In a recent programme of 'experimental archaeology', staff and volunteers have used ancient tools to saw and cleave oak planks, and in doing so have learned more about the skills of the Tudor shipwrights.

Massive wooden brackets called 'knees' were used to strengthen the hull. They spread the load at the point where deck beams meet the hull. To make them as strong as possible, they were hewn from single pieces of oak, usually the 'L' shaped section of the tree where a lower branch joins the trunk. To do this, the shipwrights had to find trees of the correct shape.

EXCAVATION, SALVAGE & CONSERVATION

When the *Mary Rose* capsized and sank, she came to rest on the sea floor on her starboard side. The hull quickly filled with silts which protected the starboard half. The exposed port side was gradually eroded by currents and eaten away by marine organisms. Over time, the remains of the *Mary Rose* and her contents were completely buried in the seabed.

The *Mary Rose* was rediscovered using sonar equipment. Every cubic centimetre of the ship was then carefully excavated by divers, most of them volunteers giving their spare time. They used their hands, or small trowels, to uncover the precious artefacts, carefully recording the position of every item found - just like on a land dig. 'Spoil' was passed to the airlift, which acted like a giant underwater vacuum cleaner and carried the unwanted silt down tide.

Visibility was very poor, usually less than 2 metres (6ft), and the divers never saw the whole structure. To avoid decompression sickness (the bends), they could only spend 96 minutes a day on the seabed. As the excavation went deeper into the hull,

the maximum diving time reduced to 46 minutes.

Fittingly, one of the last items recovered, the ship's bell, was probably one of the first to be taken on board. It has an inscription which translates as 'I was made in the year 1510' - which was when the *Mary Rose* was being built.

After the hull was salvaged and towed triumphantly into Portsmouth Royal Dockyard, it was placed in No 3 Dock, only metres from where it had been built. A temporary ship hall was built over the dock, and conservation scientists started trials to establish the best methods of preserving the ancient water-logged timbers. Archaeologists meticulously recorded the structure, and replaced timbers which had been removed underwater.

The ship hall is now an enormous laboratory where visitors can see the conservation process taking place from enclosed galleries. Since 1994, the ship has been sprayed with a water-soluble wax, polyethylene glycol, which penetrates the wood. The process will take at least 17 years and will preserve the *Mary Rose* for all time.

COMING UP

Special methods had to be developed to salvage a wreck as old and fragile as the *Mary Rose*.

Divers tunnelled under the hull to fix steel bolts in holes drilled at carefully selected points.

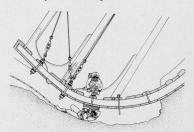

Wires connected these bolts to a lifting frame above, which was then slowly jacked up until the hull was just clear of the seabed. Suspended from the frame, the hull was transferred underwater into a cradle, which had been built to fit the shape of the hull.

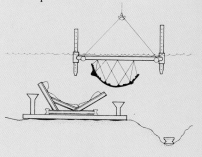

On 11 October 1982, over 60 million people around the world watched on live television as the huge crane, *Tog Mor*, lifted the whole package of 570 tonnes to the surface.

Video films in the *Mary Rose* Museum show footage of the latest diving on the wreck site.

Differences in status and wealth are reflected in the personal possessions found on board the *Mary Rose*. Ordinary sailors used wooden vessels lined with pitch, such as stave-built serving flagons and drinking tankards. These simple items contrast with valuable pewter flagons and tankards, bearing the initials or crests of their wealthy owners and the touch marks of their makers.

Many examples of personal possessions can be seen in the Mary Rose Museum, such as embroidered pouches, intricately carved and painted pocket sundials, sets of rosary beads, and finely cut combs that were vital for removing head-lice!

The *Mary Rose* paints a vivid picture of life in Tudor times. An extraordinary range of 19,000 objects were protected for over 430 years in the fine silts of the Solent. These include items you would expect to find in a great warship, like heavy bronze guns and the shot they fired, but the real treasures are the simple everyday objects which tell us about the brave men who lived and worked on board - how they cooked and what they ate, what they wore and how they spent their spare time.

Some artefacts are unique - for instance, the 137 complete longbows and 3,500 arrows are the only examples to survive from Tudor times. Others, including the magnificent

collection of pewter, are vitally important because they provide a key date for comparison with other, less well documented collections.

Swift burial within soft, butter-like, silt ensured the preservation of materials such as wood, leather, silk, wool, and bone. Everyday objects made of these materials in the 16th century rarely survive elsewhere. Many finds were tiny: peppercorns (used to relieve flatulence as well as to spice up the food), seeds, remains of insects and a rat, dice, coins, thimbles, quill pens, ink pots, pins - and thousands more.

Each of the bronze guns is unique because the mould had to be broken after the gun was cast. Their decorations differ, but all are embellished with the royal coat of arms and a variation of Henry VIII's name or initials. They may be weapons of destruction, but they are also works of art.

The bronze guns were muzzle-loaders, cast by some of the best continental gun founders, specially head-hunted by Henry VIII. As the powder and shot were loaded from the front, they had to be drawn back from the gun ports for reloading. They had a range of about 2,000m (2,230yds), but were only accurate to about 350m (385yds).

The *Mary Rose* also had wrought iron, breech-loading guns of more traditional design. Being loaded from the back, they did not have to be withdrawn from the gun port to be reloaded. They lacked the range of the bronze muzzle-loaders, but they could fire rapidly and were more devastating when fired at close range.

Different types of shot were used for different purposes: stone, lead or iron balls for shattering hulls; spike shot for bringing down rigging; and scattering shot - such as iron dice or flakes of flint in canisters - for crippling the opposing crew.

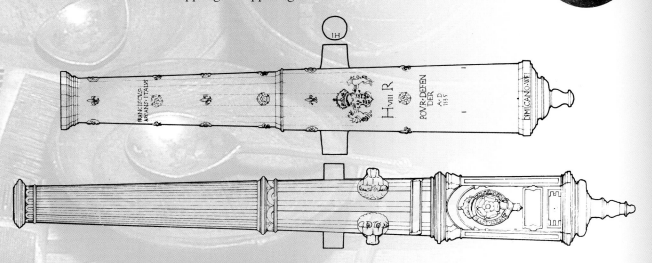

A fully illustrated Mary Rose guide book can be purchased in the Mary Rose Gift Shop
Visit the award-winning Mary Rose website at www.maryrose.org

THE GREAT

Throughout the 18th century, the Royal Navy grew in size and influence until, by 1800, it was by far the largest single employer in Britain. In 1804, there were 115 battleships and 423 smaller ships manned by some 150,000 officers and men. This seagoing force was supported by a large Dockyard work force and civil service.

Experiments in design led to the establishment of a system of 'rates', whereby ships were classified according to the number of guns and men that they carried. Standardisation of this nature made the provision of supplies and spare gear much easier.

Top of the list were the 100-gun, three-decked first rates, such as Nelson's famous flagship HMS *Victory*. With some 850 officers and men on board, these were expensive ships to run, and there were only a few in commission at any one time. More common were the workhorses of the fleet, the two-decked 74-gun third rates with their complements of about 500. At the bottom of the list were the fast frigates, single-decked sixth rates - and a large number of non-rated specialist ships such as gunboats and bomb vessels.

The men who served in these ships had to endure conditions that seem dreadful to us. But they did not think so. Food and drink were plentiful and regular. Discipline was stern, but not unduly harsh by the standards of the day. Even the infamous press gangs were largely accepted as a crude but effective means of 'persuading' experienced seamen to face danger

The Battle of Quiberon Bay, 1759

	1700	1710	1720	1730	1740	1750
Society & Technology	Industrial Revolution begins Newton's Law of Gravity	First practical steam engine Defoe's *Robinson Crusoe*	J. S. Bach		Wallpaper fashionable Handel	Rules of cricket agreed Chippendale's furniture
War & Politics	War of Spanish Succession Blenheim England & Scotland unite	Walpole - first Prime Minister		War of Austrian Succession	Culloden - last battle on British soil	Seven Years Wa
Royal Navy	Gibraltar captured Battle of Malaga				French twice defeated off Finisterre Anson's circumnavigation - first since Drake	
Portsmouth Dockyard	Great Ship Basin Main (Victory) Gate Porter's Lodge		The Naval Academy - forerunner of Dartmouth			

14

AGE OF SAIL

HMS Daedalus, an 18th Century frigate

Admiral Sir George Pocock wearing the first naval officer's uniform

and possible death in the Royal Navy - rather like the conscription employed in the last two world wars.

So, far from being the cowed jailbirds often portrayed in films and novels, the 18th century sailors were a proud, disciplined and highly-skilled body of men.

Their calibre was strikingly shown in the string of successes which Britain achieved at sea in the long wars against revolutionary France and Napoleon between 1793 and 1815. This was a huge conflict, involving every European power and even the newly-independent USA. A whole generation grew up in the shadow of war and battles were fought all over the world. It had been preceded by a century of almost continuous conflict - 5 major wars,

totalling 38 years, mostly against France - in which the Royal Navy had developed into Britain's main strategic force. Long experience of war at sea had created a service of unique skill and professionalism. As a result, the British won a series of decisive victories under leaders such as Howe, Jervis, Duncan - and, of course, Nelson.

Not all battles were large fleet actions such as Trafalgar. There were many single-ship and small squadron contests and boat actions that carried the war right into opponents' home territory, and much effort was devoted to blockading their ports. In every part of the known world, the Royal Navy captured colonies, thus cutting off enemy trade and increasing Britain's wealth.

Sea power, on its own, could not defeat a major land power such as France. But the British victory at sea was an essential first step, without which the eventual defeat of Napoleon could not have happened. It was the Royal Navy's Golden Age, when it established for itself a reputation for invincibility that it has never really lost.

Founded in 1911, the Royal Naval Museum is one of the oldest maritime museums in the country. Outstanding collections and imaginative interactives combine to present a comprehensive and dynamic portrait of the Navy in the Great Age of Sail, culminating in 'The Trafalgar Experience'.

	1760	1770	1780	1790	1800	1815
	Voltaire Robert Adam	Adam Smith	Mozart	Jenner's smallpox vaccination		Slave trade abolished
	Watt's steam engine	Spinning Jenny	First iron bridge	French Revolution	Volta demonstrates electricity	Goethe	Beethoven
	Wolfe's victory at Quebec	War of American Independence		War with France and Spain	Austerlitz Retreat from Moscow	
	Clive triumphs in India		New South Wales settled	Napoleon I	Wagram Vittoria	Waterloo
	French defeated at Quiberon Bay		*Bounty* sails from Portsmouth	'The Glorious First of June'	Cape St Vincent Trafalgar	War of 1812 v USA. Mixed
	HMS *Victory*'s keel laid				The Nile	fortunes. White House burnt.
		Great Storehouses Cook returns from second exploration	Arson attack on Great Rope House		Block Mills	Charles Dickens born -
			Admiralty House 'First Fleet' sails to Australia			father works in Pay Office

Admiralty House was built in 1786 as the residence of the Dockyard Commissioner. Now the official residence of the Second Sea Lord, every monarch since George III has stayed in it. It also boasts one of the first flush toilets!

The Great Rope House, which turned out mile after mile of essential rigging, was the victim of several fires, most famously when set alight in 1776 by 'Jack the Painter', a Scot supporting the cause of American independence. He was hanged from the frigate *Arethusa's* 20m (65ft) mizzen mast, which was specially mounted just inside Victory Gate so that the culprit could contemplate his folly as his life expired. As its name implies, Anchor Lane, which runs alongside the Rope House, was where anchors were stored. Hemp, for making the rope, was kept in the storehouses opposite.

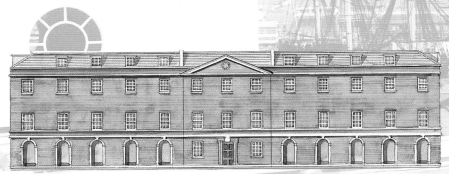

Storehouse No. 9 1784

THE WORLD'S GREATEST INDUSTRIAL COMPLEX

When France replaced the Dutch Republic as Britain's main competitor for world trade, the theatre of conflict moved from the North Sea to the Channel and the open oceans. This gave tremendous impetus to Portsmouth Royal Dockyard, with its sheltered location on the south coast, and during the 18th century it developed into the greatest industrial complex in the world.

The hub was the Great Ship Basin - which, being tide-free, made it much easier to service ships - and the Great Stone Dock, the oldest surviving dry dock in the world. They date from 1698.

Many of the buildings near the Great Ship Basin date from the second half of the 18th century, a period of almost continuous naval warfare. The three Great Storehouses, shown below, were built between 1760 and 1790 and kept an enormous range of provisions from iron and copper nails, to brooms and holystones, to complete sets of rigging. Their interior structures are largely built of re-used ship timbers. The clock tower is a replica of the original which was destroyed in an air raid in 1941.

A town within a town, the Dockyard also boasted fine houses, a church, schools for apprentices, a mortuary, beer bars, shops, surgeries, and a fire station.

The Great Ship Basin and the Block Mills

During the Napoleonic wars, the Dockyard was at the leading edge of the industrial revolution. A steam engine was installed in 1799 to pump water from the dry docks, and three years later steam power was used to drive one of the first mechanical saw mills. The world's first steam dredger was built to dig an extension to the Great Basin, and in 1802, the world's first caisson (pronounced kas-soon) was installed at the entrance to the newly enhanced dock complex. It could be filled with water and sunk into the dock entrance to provide a watertight seal. When it had to be moved, it was pumped free of water and refloated.

These achievements were overshadowed by the opening of the Block Mills in 1803. It was the world's first completely steam-powered factory. The block making machinery, designed by Marc Brunel - father of Isambard Kingdom - turned out 130,000 pulley blocks a year for the rigging of ships like HMS *Victory*. Thirty unskilled men using the 45 machines could equal the output of 100 skilled craftsmen. The Block Mills can be seen from the stern of HMS *Victory*, and some of the pioneering machinery is on display in the Dockyard Apprentice Exhibition.

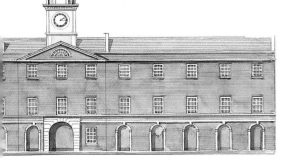

Storehouse No. 10 1776

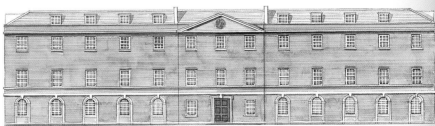

Storehouse No. 11 1764

FACTS AND FIGURES

Overall length:	69.2m (227ft)
Length on gun deck:	56.7m (186ft)
Beam:	16m (52ft)
Displacement:	3,600 tonnes (3,500 tons)
Total length of rigging:	45km (27 miles)
Max speed:	8 knots (9 mph)
Timber used (mainly oak):	About 40ha (100 acres) of woodland
Cost of construction:	£63,176
Storage of provisions:	940 tonnes (920 tons)

Armament at Trafalgar:

Lower deck	30 x 32-pounders
Middle deck	28 x 24-pounders
Upper deck	30 x long 12-pounders
Quarter deck	12 x short 12-pounders
Forecastle	2 x 68-pounder carronades
	2 x medium 12-pounders

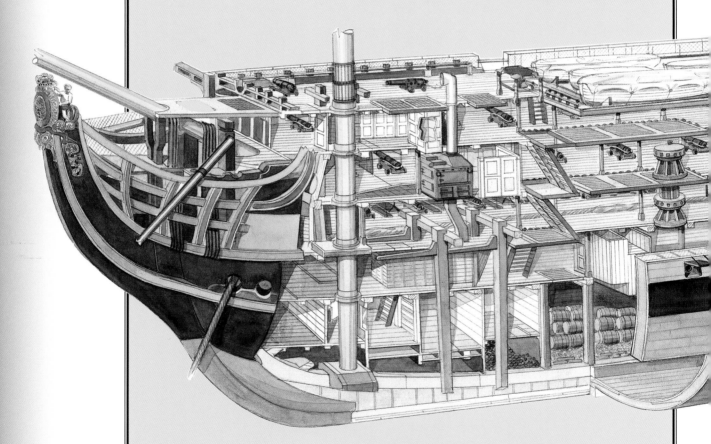

Crew at Trafalgar:

821, made up of:
11 officers (including Nelson).
48 non-commissioned officers (including master, bosun, surgeon, gunner, carpenter, purser, cook etc and 22 midshipmen).
80 petty officers, 204 able seamen, 195 ordinary seamen, 90 landsmen, 40 boys.
4 Royal Marine officers, 149 Marines.

HMS VICTORY
The World's Greatest Warship

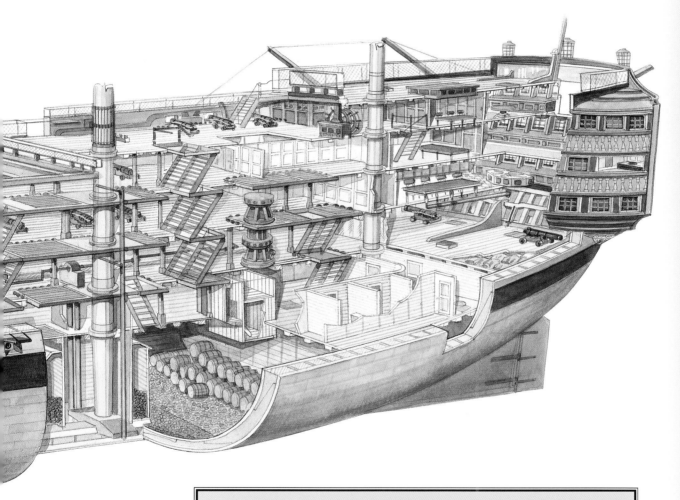

The galleries at the stern: Captain Hardy's at the top, Lord Nelson's in the middle, and the officer's wardroom at the bottom. In preparation for battle, the interior bulkheads (partitions) and furniture were removed and guns installed. Above is the poop deck, from which Nelson commanded the fleet.

The World's Oldest Commissioned Warship

1759
Keel laid at Chatham

1765
Completed, but put into reserve

1778
Commissioned as flagship of Admiral Keppel
after outbreak of the American War of Independence

1780
Bottom plated with 3,923 copper sheets, weighing 17 tonnes

12 December 1781
Admiral Kempenfelt's flagship at his victory off Ushant

1782
Flagship of Admiral Howe at the Relief of Gibraltar

1793
Flagship of Lord Hood, Commander-in-Chief, Mediterranean

14 February 1797
Flagship of Admiral Sir John Jervis at his triumph at Cape St. Vincent

1800-1803
The 'Great Repair'

1803
Sails for Mediterranean as Nelson's flagship

21 October 1805
Battle of Trafalgar. Death of Nelson

1808-1812
Flagship for campaigns in the Baltic

1824
Flagship of the Port Admiral at Portsmouth

1831
Reprieved by 1st Sea Lord Admiral Sir Thomas Hardy
(*Victory's* captain at Trafalgar), at his wife's insistence

1889
Flagship of Commander-in-Chief, Portsmouth

12 January 1922
Brought into dry dock for preservation

1928
Re-opens to the public

1941
Damaged when a bomb falls between the dock and the hull

The spot where Nelson fell

Nelson enjoyed a sumptuous suite of rooms with day, dining and sleeping cabins, plus servants' space. Those of his captain, Thomas Hardy, were only a little less luxurious.

Temeraire   Redoutable   HMS *Victory*

LORD NELSON'S FLAGSHIP

The flagship of the new Commander-in-Chief of the Mediterranean fleet was looking as good as new as she set sail from Portsmouth on 20 May 1803. Resplendent in a new black and yellow livery, and boasting a new figurehead, HMS *Victory* was fresh from a three year refit in which she underwent considerable rebuilding.

Already famed as the veteran flagship of great triumphs at Ushant and Cape St Vincent, and of distinguished admirals such as Keppel, Kempenfelt, Howe, Hood, and Jervis, *Victory's* greatest moment was still to come. The vice-admiral whose flag was flying at her fore topmast that day, Viscount Horatio Nelson KB, would achieve such fame for his exploits in HMS *Victory* that it would dwarf that of his illustrious predecessors.

Victory looks much the same today as then, and still flies an admiral's flag, that of the Second Sea Lord, Commander-in-Chief, Naval Home Command. Her tranquillity in retirement, however, is a far cry from the noise and exertion of the 821 officers and men who crowded into *Victory* when Nelson set sail from Portsmouth in search of battle.

Below: A Section of The Panorama of The Battle of Trafalgar 1930: W. L. Wyllie as seen in the Victory Gallery.

Left: W.L Wyllie and his daughter, Aileen, at work on the Panorama in 1930.

For 18 months he blockaded the French Fleet in Toulon, before chasing it all the way to the West Indies and back, only to see it find refuge in the Spanish port of Cadiz. Finally, on 19 October 1805, the French Admiral Pierre de Villeneuve, acting on Napoleon's instructions, ordered the combined Franco-Spanish fleet to set sail for the Mediterranean.

After shadowing it for two days, Nelson attacked off Cape Trafalgar on the south west coast of Spain. *Victory*, leading one of two parallel columns of British warships, headed for the French flagship *Bucentaure*. A single devastating broadside crippled the *Bucentaure* and left the Franco-Spanish fleet floundering without a leader. The 74-gun *Redoutable*, sandwiched between *Victory* and the equally formidable British *Temeraire*, put up a sterner fight, her captain and crew demonstrating extraordinary skill and courage. At the height of the battle, one of her marksmen mortally wounded Nelson as he paced *Victory's* quarter-deck.

After the battle, a battered *Victory* was towed to Gibraltar for makeshift repairs, then limped back to England with Nelson's body preserved in a barrel of brandy in preparation for a hero's funeral.

Santissima Trinidad   Neptune

Battle of Trafalgar
12·45p.m. 21st October 1805

THE FIGHTING MACHINE

A 100-gun, first-rate ship-of-the-line, *Victory* was designed to deliver shattering broadsides from batteries of guns arranged on three decks. She was a fighting machine, but in those days before mechanisation, a machine that ran on muscle power.

Every one of the 821 officers and crew on Nelson's *Victory* knew their place in the machine. Nelson's job was to direct the fleet. The ship itself was run by Captain Hardy from his cabin on the quarter-deck, a few steps from his command post. Reporting to him was a team of lieutenants, each with a specific area of responsibility such as signalling or gunnery and assisted by trainee officers called midshipmen. The remaining officers were specialists like the purser, responsible for supplies, and the master, in charge of navigation.

Most of the crew were either able or ordinary seamen, who were experienced sailors, or novice landsmen. It included boys as young as ten, many of them orphans sent to sea to learn a trade. About half the crew were volunteers. The rest were conscripted, either through the 'quota', by which counties and seaports had to supply a certain number of men for the Navy, or the press gang. Lastly, there was a unit of 153 Royal Marines to provide accurate musket fire in battle.

Some 500 crew lived on the lower gun deck. The gun ports were usually kept closed, so it was dark, damp and smelly. Not surprisingly, rheumatism was a common complaint. There were fifteen 32-pounder guns on each side, each pair manned by a crew of 15. In battle, 'powder monkeys' - men and boys - kept them supplied with powder charges from the magazine below. Hammocks, each allowed 400mm (16in) width, were slung from the beams, and mess tables were placed between the guns and along the deck. Food and drink rations were generous, with three meals a day. Breakfast comprised cold oatmeal porridge, dinner was a salted meat stew cooked in the galley, and supper was biscuits and cheese. This was washed down with half a pint of rum mixed with water, issued in two parts - half at midday and half in the evening.

Discipline was strict. For insolence or disobedience, for example, a man could be sentenced to up to two dozen lashes with a 'cat o' nine tails', administered in front of the whole crew on the upper deck.

The capstan was used for hoisting heavy loads such as sails, the ship's boats, supplies, and the four mighty anchors. Up to 200 men could be used for the heaviest loads, with 10 men pushing with their chests against each capstan bar.

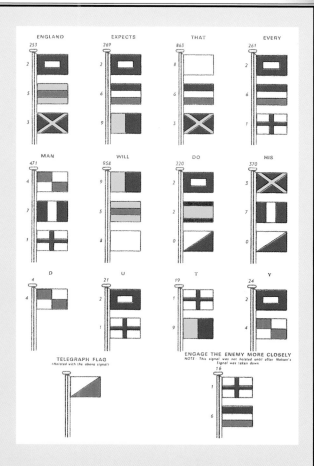

ENGLAND EXPECTS THAT EVERY MAN WILL DO HIS DUTY

Each year on Trafalgar Day, 21 October, Nelson's immortal signal 'England Expects…' is flown from *Victory's* masts. The three masts are - from bow to stern - fore mast, main mast and mizzen mast. The full height of the main mast from the waterline is 62.5m (205ft). 22.8m (75ft) up from the deck is the main top, a platform used by sharpshooters in battle - 40 at a time. Just below it is the main yard, 31m (102ft) wide. and weighing 7 tonnes (7 tons). 32 different sails were used in different combinations, depending on the weather. They were adjusted by complex arrangements of ropes and pulleys.

Victory's original, very elaborate, figurehead commemorating the 'Year of Victories', 1759 - the year her keel was laid - was removed during her 1803 refit. Its replacement was much simpler: the coat of arms of King George III supported by a cherub and a seraph.

This replica of Victory's *original figurehead can be seen in the Victory Gallery*

Victory afloat in Portsmouth Harbour at the end of the 19th Century

Arguably the most famous sea battle ever, and certainly one of the most decisive, the Battle of Trafalgar took place on 21st October 1805. Off the coast of south-west Spain, 27 British ships, brilliantly led by Vice Admiral Lord Nelson in his flagship, HMS *Victory*, crushed a combined French and Spanish fleet of 33 ships. 19 of the enemy's battleships either surrendered or were destroyed; at least 7,000 of the 30,000 men on the French and Spanish side were killed or wounded, as against 1,600 on the British side.

Trafalgar destroyed forever any ambitions the French Emperor Napoleon may have had of invading Britain and it ushered in a century of British domination of the sea.

But for the sailors who took part, and, when the news reached Britain, for the country at large, joy at such a great victory was overshadowed by sadness at the death of Nelson. Shot by a sniper from the rigging of the French ship *Redoutable*, early in the battle, Nelson survived long enough to learn of the British triumph.

200 years after his death, Horatio Nelson is still a major British hero. His special gift for inspiring leadership has never been surpassed and he won for himself a place in British hearts that he retains to this day.

Born in Burnham Thorpe, Norfolk on 29 September 1758, he went to sea at the age of 12 and rose rapidly to become a Captain at only 21. He showed his mettle early and was rewarded by senior commands when he was still in his 30s.

Although well-known in the Navy as a rising star, it was not until he was 38 that he captured the imagination of the British public. At the Battle of Cape St. Vincent (1797), he personally led a boarding party that captured two Spanish battleships, thus earning himself a place in the storybooks.

A unique run of decisive victories followed: against the French at the Nile (1798), the Danes at Copenhagen (1801) and, his swan-song and masterpiece, Trafalgar (1805). These

NELSON AT THE ROYAL NAVAL MUSEUM

The Royal Naval Museum has one of the best collections of Nelson material in the world. It includes fine portraits and items, such as his uniform, the furniture from his cabin in HMS *Victory*, and pieces from his collection of silver plate, amassed by an American citizen Mrs Lily McCarthy. The core of the collection is very personal - private relics lovingly preserved by the descendants of his daughter Horatia. These include his watch, the miniature of Emma Hamilton that he wore round his neck, and even locks of his hair.

successes came at times when the war was going badly elsewhere for Britain and her allies, and made him an international hero.

Mourned by the whole nation, he was given a state funeral in St. Paul's Cathedral. Demand for mementoes of the hero was so great that the market was flooded with souvenirs, many of which still survive - the Royal Naval Museum has one of the finest collections.

With his empty sleeve and sightless eye, Nelson looked a hero and, although he always had an air of frailty,

he was a man of great vitality and enthusiasm, with a special gift for inspiring others - witness his famous signal made just before battle was joined at Trafalgar, 'England expects that every man will do his duty'. He was a skilled tactician and master strategist but it was his human qualities which made him so many friends. He is also remembered for his very public affair with one of the most beautiful women of the day, Emma, Lady Hamilton.

As one of his officers put it, 'Nelson was the man to love!'

The Trafalgar Experience: as seen in the Royal Naval Museum's Victory Gallery. In the same gallery, visitors can find out if they had an ancestor at the Battle of Trafalgar in the 'Who was at Trafalgar?' display.

What did Nelson look like?

The Royal Naval Museum's Nelson figure, a 1998 view, based on the latest research and evidence, shows Nelson just before Trafalgar in 1805.

Simon de Koster's portrait based on a sketch drawn at Nelson's house in December 1800. Nelson thought it "the most like me." Emma Hamilton kept a copy in a locket.

Nelson, painted in Vienna in 1800 by Heinrich Füger during his triumphant tour of Europe with Sir William and Lady Emma Hamilton.

A naval gun crew in the Sudan in 1884, the origin of the famous naval field gun runs which continue to this day. Sailors often had to go ashore to look after Her Majesty's interests - indeed, the rifles and revolvers seen on HMS *Warrior* were mainly for arming such parties.

TUG OF WAR!

The first steam ships were paddle steamers. When screw propellers were introduced, trials were carried out at Portsmouth to establish which was the better form of propulsion. In the most famous of the tests, on 3 April 1845, the screw propeller steamer *Rattler* decisively beat the paddle steamer *Alecto* in a tug of war. *Rattler's* winning propeller is displayed in the colonnade outside the Royal Naval Museum.

*T*he 19th century was a time of revolutionary technological and social change for the Royal Navy.

First came steam-power. Introduced initially in small ships, it spread quickly until, eventually, a whole fleet of splendid sail-and-steam wooden battleships had been created. Then these too were swept away by the advent of the armoured iron battleship HMS *Warrior*. The most revolutionary warship ever built, she rendered every other battleship obsolete. However, the rate of change in technology that she introduced was so fast that she herself was obsolete within a few years.

An experimental period followed when the Royal Navy comprised a bewildering kaleidoscope of greatly differing designs. Eventually, however, around 1890, a single design emerged and a splendid fleet of modern battleships was constructed.

	1815	1820	1830	1840	1850
Society & Technology	Jane Austen Byron	Faraday's dynamo Turner Stephenson's *Locomotion*	Slavery abolished in British Empire	Irish famine Marx The Great Exhibition Anaesthetics first used	
War & Politics	Congress of Vienna Peterloo massacre	Belgian independence Reform Act Queen Victoria	Napoleon III Revolution across Europe Crimean War		
Royal Navy	First Royal Navy steam ship Last sail battle - Navarino	Hong Kong taken *Rattler* vs *Alecto* contest	First official sailor's uniform		
Portsmouth Dockyard	Gas lighting HMS *Fox* - first steam warship built in Portsmouth	First Fleet Review by Queen Victoria	First great expansion Last timber hull built		

OF STEAM

Innovation was not limited to capital ships. Mines, torpedoes, submarines, wireless: all such aspects of a modern fleet were first developed in these inventive years. At the same time the principal dockyards were greatly enlarged, and their skills extended to enable them to service the new fleet. An extensive network of coaling stations was established to enable the steamships to operate anywhere in the world.

The men, and the conditions in which they lived, changed dramatically too. Seamen were employed for a fixed period and given proper training, thus having an assured career for the first time. Specialist branches emerged to master the new skills, such as engineering. Regular wages, pensions, and many other social improvements ensured that the Navy began to offer an attractive career.

The period was known as the Pax Britannica (the British peace) and Britain only became involved in one major international war - the Crimean War with Russia (1854-56). But it was also a time of expansion; British merchant ships dominated the trade routes of the world, and Britain continually extended its overseas Empire. Furthermore, the Royal Navy played a key role in the suppression of the slave trade. Such activity frequently caused conflict and so, in fact, the era was far from peaceful.

Throughout the century, the Royal Navy maintained squadrons in all corners of the world. In 1870, of the 113 ships in commission only 22 were in home waters; the rest were dispersed abroad. As a result, the Navy was often first on the spot when trouble broke out and so the average bluejacket saw plenty of action. There were numerous small-scale wars in which sailors served as boatmen on rivers, and fought alongside the soldiers and Royal Marines ashore.

There were no great battles and glorious victories in this period but it marked, nonetheless, the very peak of the Royal Navy's power and influence.

HMS Kent, a late Victorian armoured cruiser

	1860		1870			1880			1890		1900
	Football Association		Mass production of steel		Electric lighting	Impressionists	Gilbert & Sullivan		Marconi's wireless	First modern Olympiad	
arwin		Transatlantic telegraph cable		FA Cup	Bell's telephone		Dunlop's pneumatic tyres		Forth Bridge	Moving pictures	Marie Curie
	Italian unification	First dominion- Canada		Bismarck unifies Germany		Zulu Wars					Second Boer War
	American Civil War		Suez Canal	Victoria- Empress of India		Gladstone & Disraeli					
	HMS *Warrior*									Naval Brigade fights	
	Moustaches banned			Abolition of flogging		Bombardment of Alexandria				in South Africa	
	Second great expansion		HMS *Devastation, Inflexible, Colossus*						HMS *Havock*	HMS *Formidable*	
'Palmerston's follies' - Solent forts			Respectively, first battleships without sails, with electricity, of steel.						First destroyer	First million pound battleship	

THE STEAM AND IRON DOCKYARD

Portsmouth Royal Dockyard had been built to service the needs of the great sailing ships, but it was poorly prepared for the very different requirements of the Victorian steam fleet.

Firmly entrapped by the fortifications of Portsea, the only way for the Dockyard to expand was northwards into the harbour. There, a huge new enclosed basin was constructed, along with three new dry docks, engine and boiler factories, foundries and one of the world's largest steam smitheries. Queen Victoria opened the new complex on 25 May 1848, watched by a crowd of 15,000. It was the biggest and most modern naval facility in the world.

Within 15 years it had been outdated. A new breed of leviathan battleship, led by HMS *Warrior*, had arrived. Further expansion was needed.

In 1864, the Admiralty was authorised to reclaim 73 hectares (180 acres) from mudlands and part of Portsea Common. They used it to construct four basins, three dry docks, two locks, 4.5km (5,000 yds) of wharfage, plus new armour-plate workshops. Millions of tonnes of earth and shingle were excavated and moved to create an island in the harbour called Whale Island, which became the home of the Royal Navy's foremost gunnery school. Over 155 million bricks were made on site for the foundations of the docks. Quarries in Devon and Cornwall supplied millions of tons of granite and stone. It was one of the largest engineering projects ever undertaken in Britain.

The opening of the new complex in 1876 coincided with the launch of HMS *Inflexible*, the world's largest battleship. The first major warship to be fitted throughout with electric lighting and the first to be launched using electricity, it was yet another world record for Portsmouth Royal Dockyard.

The great Victorian development is the heart of the modern Naval Base. At the upper left is the expansion of 1843, and at the upper right is the expansion of 1864

The conventional brick facade of No 6 Boathouse, built in 1848, gives no clue to the amazing iron structure inside. A triumph of Victorian engineering, Boathouse 6 is now home to ACTION STATIONS.

1. Figure head
2. Diagram of rigging (on the jetty)
3. Armoured conning tower
4. 110-pounder 'stern chaser' gun
5. Navigating bridge
6. Upper deck - capstan
7. Crew's 'heads' (toilets)
8. Cable deck - petty officers' messes & livestock manger
9. Main gun deck
10. Galley
11. Desk from which ship's routine was run
12. Action steering position
13. Captain's cabin
14. Commissioned officers' wardroom
15. Compartment for junior officers' chests
16. Provision issue room and emergency steering wheels
17. Rum!
18. Funnel uptakes & sailors' kit bag stowage
19. Laundry
20. Boiler rooms
21. Engine room
22. Cells

The numbers can be found on signs around the ship and tie in with a 'Sound Alive' hand held guide which can be hired at the Warrior reception desk.

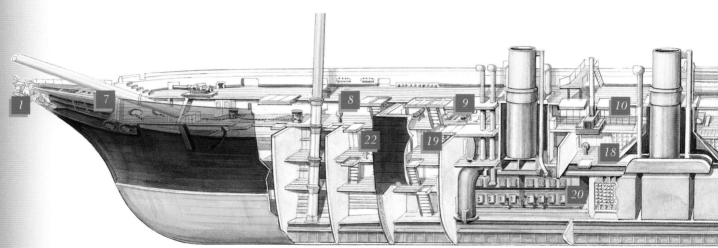

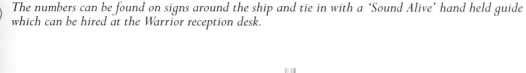

The core of HMS *Warrior's* design was the 'citadel', a 64.6m (210ft) long 'armoured box' which protected her guns and machinery. It was impenetrable by the latest guns, even at close range. The bow and stern of the ship were not armour-plated. *Warrior* was divided into watertight compartments to limit the spread of water if the ship was holed, a recent innovation only made possible by her iron construction.

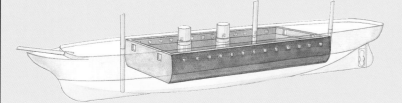

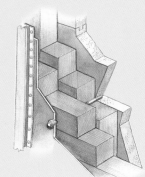

The citadel's side armour-plating was made of 114mm (4.5in) of wrought iron plate backed with 450mm (18in) of teak. It weighed 1,325 tonnes (1,300 tons) in total, one-seventh of the ship's total weight.

HMS WARRIOR
1860
'The Black Snake'

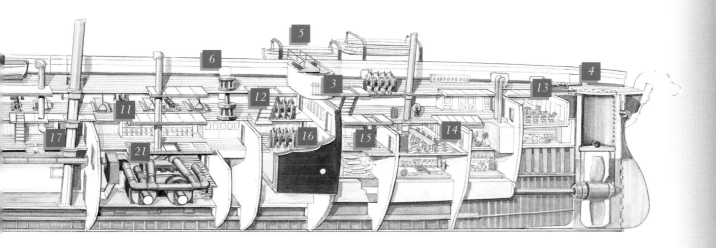

FACTS AND FIGURES

Overall length:	127m (418ft)
Beam:	18m (58ft)
Draught:	8m (26ft) at full load
Displacement:	9,367 tonnes (9,200 tons)
Top speed under steam:	14 .33 knots (about 16mph/26kph)
Top speed under sail:	13.75 knots (about 15mph/25kph)
Fastest speed steam & sail	17.5 knots (20.15mph/32.43kph)
Cost:	£332,000
Armament:	26 x 68-pounder muzzle loaders, range 2.5km (1.5miles)
	10 x 110-pounder breech loaders, range 4.5km (2.7miles)
	4 x 40-pounder breech loaders, range 3km (1.9miles)
Crew:	705, made up of:
	22 officers, 20 midshipmen.
	3 warrant officers, 54 non-commissioned officers.
	401 seamen and boys.
	2 chief engineers, 10 engineers, 66 stokers and trimmers.
	3 Royal Marine officers, 6 NCOs, 118 artillerymen.

A Pioneering Battleship

25 May 1859
Keel laid

29 December 1860
Launched

24 October 1861
Accepted into the Navy
Joins the Channel Squadron, patrolling 'home waters' from Gibraltar to Scandinavia

1863
Visited by 270,000 people on a 12 week flag showing tour around Britain

1864-1867
First major refit

1867-1871
Channel Squadron

1869
Tows floating dock to Bermuda

1871- 1875
Second major refit in Portsmouth

1875
Relegated to the First Reserve (the 'Coastguard')

1883
Enters Portsmouth under steam for the last time

Laid up in dockyard reserve in 'Rotten Row', a remote corner of Portsmouth Harbour

1904-1924
Part of HMS *Vernon*, the Navy's electrical school afloat

1929
Becomes a floating jetty for an oil fuel depot at Milford Haven, Wales

1968
First proposals for restoration

1979
Towed to Hartlepool

16 June 1987
Arrives Portsmouth after restoration

THE ULTIMATE DETERRENT

When completed in 1861, HMS *Warrior* was the world's largest, fastest, most heavily armed, most heavily armoured, warship. No opponent dared challenge her.

Warrior was built to counter the threat of France's Emperor Napoleon III. Hankering to emulate the military glories of his uncle, he ordered a fleet of steam-propelled battleships. The plans for the first, *La Gloire*, caused consternation in Britain because iron armour-plating was to be added to its wooden hull, making it the world's first 'ironclad'.

Concern escalated when Queen Victoria and Prince Albert found French war preparations in full swing on their goodwill visit to Cherbourg in August 1858. Albert fumed that the British government was not taking the threat seriously enough.

The Royal Navy had already put steam engines in some wooden line-of-battleships. Generally, however, these ships were only bigger versions of HMS *Victory*. The Admiralty considered following the example of *La Gloire* by simply adding iron plates to conventional wooden ships. After much agonising, however, it went for the more radical option of battleships with hulls made of iron.

The contract to build the first was awarded to the Thames Iron Works & Shipbuilding Company of Blackwall, London. 'I wonder how I mustered sufficient courage to order the construction of such a vessel', mused the First Lord of the Admiralty. 'I wonder how I mustered sufficient courage to undertake it', replied the director of the yard!

Their trepidation was justified. The Press relished telling stories of delay and mounting cost, although they were inevitable given the pioneering nature of the work, and the Admiralty had to step in to prevent the yard going bankrupt. Nevertheless, *Warrior* came off the slip after only 18 months and, after fitting out and trials, was accepted into the Navy on 24 October 1861.

Warrior instantly made all other warships obsolete. Combining for the first time an iron hull, a steam engine and armour-plating, she was the world's first modern battleship and the epitome of Victorian Britain's technological prowess. She could out-run and out-gun any existing battleship, and her long sleek lines made them all look old fashioned. *Warrior* was a superstar, the subject of enormous interest both at home and abroad. Napoleon III described her as 'a black snake amongst rabbits' - his ambitions had been thwarted.

Warrior was the progenitor of the 'Black Battle Fleet' of the 1860s and 1870s. By 1875, Britain had built a further 22 armour-plated iron battleships, the latest with 38-ton guns mounted in turrets protected by solid iron armour 360mm (14in) thick. They had no sails and could steam three times further than *Warrior* without refuelling. *Warrior* was already out of date. She had never had to fire a shot in anger - which is the true measure of her success.

Warrior's masts may seem out of place in all the new technology, but her engines were not sufficiently fuel efficient to cope without them. Burning 11 tonnes of coal an hour at full speed, *Warrior* had a steaming range of no more than 3,500km (2,000 miles), which was not, for example, enough to cross the Atlantic. The Royal Navy did not develop a world-wide network of coaling stations until the 1880s. As a result, long passages were made under sail, with steam used for manoeuvring and entering and leaving harbour. When under sail, the funnels telescoped down and the enormous propeller was hoisted clear of the water.

Warrior's ten new 110-pounder breech-loading guns were designed by Sir William Armstrong to pierce the armour-plate of ironclads. Normal round cannon balls simply bounced off armour, but Armstrong's guns fired elongated shells, which were given a spin so that they went straight and faster. *Warrior* was supposed to be fitted entirely with these 110-pounders, but trials were not completed in time.

Unlike wooden battleships, *Warrior* had just one gun deck. It was 100 feet longer than any previous warship, and very stable so that she was able to carry much heavier guns.

The twenty-six 68-pounders on her gun deck were of conventional design but were five times more destructive than the 32-pounders carried by wooden ships. Each gun had a crew of 18.

Warrior had 10 boilers, each with four furnaces. At full power, the temperature reached 40°C (100°F), but under easy steam it was no more than 'pleasantly warm'. 'Trimmers' shovelled coal from the bunkers to the furnaces, using small trucks on rails which were nicknamed the GWR - 'Great Warrior Railway'. 'Stokers' shovelled the coal into the furnaces, and removed white hot ash and clinker which they doused with water and hoisted to the upper deck to be poured over the side.

LIVING IN A CROWD

Six hundred men lived on the gun deck. Their job was to man the guns and provide muscle power for other tasks. Although *Warrior* was a step change in naval design from *Victory*, she still lacked powered machinery to do backbreaking tasks like hoisting six tonne yards, five and a half tonne anchors, and the 26 tonne propeller. As on *Victory*, ruptures were an occupational hazard - the medical stores contained 200 trusses! At least, however, *Warrior's* crew had a 16 piece band to encourage them as they pushed and pulled.

Hoisting such huge weights was made possible by the capstan, which was operated by up to 120 men. In operation, it looked like a densely packed human whirlpool.

When he was not hauling, a sailor was likely to be scrubbing, cleaning or polishing. The atmosphere was always damp, making tuberculosis a serious risk. After coaling ship, which entailed loading up to 850 tonnes of coal through the gun ports and down into the bunkers, it took a week of hard labour to restore the ship to its normal pristine condition.

The ship's company was divided into 34 messes, each with 18 men squashed into the area between two guns - much more space than *Victory's* crew!

They crammed around the simple mess tables at mealtimes, and at night slung their hammocks above, 710mm (28in) apart. Each mess had a rack holding a tin basin, plate and spoon for each man, and various other wooden utensils, all marked with the number of the mess. Twice weekly, members of the mess washed themselves and their clothes. They had one useful modern convenience - a laundry, the first to be installed in a Royal Navy ship.

Unlike *Victory's* sailors, *Warrior's* crew had all volunteered for a career in the Navy, the result of a reform of 1853. Most entered as boys and underwent nine months basic training before joining their ship. Other reforms had introduced uniforms and better food rations, modified the disciplinary code, and provided pensions - a rare privilege in those days.

Discipline was still tough. For minor misdemeanours, sailors might have their leave stopped, or have to do extra work and drill, or stand facing the bulkhead for hours on end. Flogging was very occasionally used to punish offences like theft and regular drunkenness at sea, but imprisonment was more usual, and *Warrior* has its own cells.

By the standards of the time, life was tolerably good.

The senior officers relaxed and took their meals in the wardroom. It was surrounded by their cabins, each 1.8m (6ft) by 3m (10ft) and furnished with a bunk, collapsible table, and washstand with basin and jug. The Captain lived in splendid isolation in his own spacious quarters, which included a day cabin used for dining and entertaining, and also his office, a pantry, and sleeping quarters.

REBIRTH

Warrior has survived partly because of the superb quality of her iron hull, and partly because of extraordinary luck. Being converted to a floating pontoon in 1929 may have been an ignominious comedown for one of the greatest ships ever built, but it did protect her for 50 years until restoration became possible.

Realising the hulk's significance, the Ship Preservation Trust (now called the Warrior Preservation Trust) took it to Hartlepool for restoration in 1979. After so many years, considerable research was needed to establish exactly what the ship had been like. Fortunately, the Royal Naval Museum unearthed the remarkable journal of Henry Murray, a 14 year old Midshipman in 1861, who had drawn plans and diagrams recording in meticulous detail all the fittings and equipment and showing where everything went.

After eight years of skilful rebuilding, made possible thanks to the generosity of one man - John Smith, HMS *Warrior* was restored to her 1861 condition and, in June 1987, returned to Portsmouth to take her rightful place of honour alongside *Mary Rose* and HMS *Victory*.

A full colour HMS Warrior guide book is available from the HMS Warrior 1860 reception desk

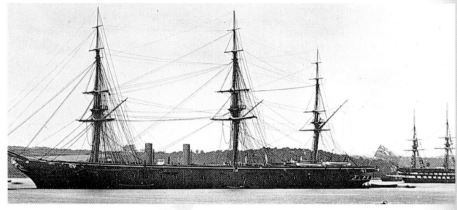

In her prime, flying the Red Ensign of the Channel Squadron in 1862...

In decline, HMS Vernon torpedo school in 1904...

Almost forgotten, Milford Haven in the 1960s... and overleaf, coming home 1987...

35

The seeds of the Royal Navy's decline were sown early in the new century, but it was not until 1945 that this decline really became apparent. By huge efforts, and with appalling loss of life, Britain twice managed to defend her position as the dominant sea power against strong challenges from Germany, only to see it finally eclipsed by the USA.

The century opened with the launch in 1906, at Portsmouth, of the revolutionary new warship, HMS *Dreadnought*. Her high speed, generated by new turbine engines, and enormous firepower from ten 12-inch guns, made all other battleships obsolete - including Britain's own, most of which were less than ten years old.

Dreadnought started a naval arms race between Britain and Germany, each building ever more powerful ships. In 1916, the two fleets clashed at Jutland. Fought on a vast scale, the battle was confused and indecisive, but afterwards the German High Seas Fleet withdrew into port and seldom ventured out again.

Although vulnerable to air attack, larger battleships continued to be built. They were still valuable weapons when used in conjunction with aircraft carriers and cruisers, a combination that proved deadly to the German battleship *Bismarck* in 1941. But the days of the huge set-piece gun duels between large battle fleets had passed.

Cruisers, faster and lighter than battleships, defended the trade routes

---

The Royal Naval Museum's Twentieth Century Exhibition in Storehouse No 10 features a special exhibition on HMS *Dreadnought* until March 2007 and then The Falklands War.

---

and, in peacetime, showed the flag overseas, promoting prestige and goodwill. At the Battle of the Falklands in 1914, British battle-cruisers

The Battle of Jutland 1916 by W Bishop

destroyed Germany's finest overseas squadron. Twenty five years later, at the Battle of the River Plate, a cruiser squadron cornered and outmanoeuvred the German pocket battleship *Graf Spee*.

However, in both world wars, the main threat to Britain's sea power came from the submarine. The skills of the German U-boat crews threatened the flow of food and vital supplies so much that in 1917, and again in 1943, Britain was nearly brought to her knees.

Many different countermeasures were tried. In World War I, the use of `Q` ships, armed ships disguised as helpless merchantmen, and direct raids on U-boat bases - such as the attack on Zeebrugge in 1918 - were only partially successful. In both wars, the most successful defence proved to be the old 'convoy' system: taking groups of merchant ships under the escort of specially-equipped small warships like the 'Flower' class corvettes of World War II. Improved technology and tactics gradually turned the tide against the U-boats and won the crucial Battle of the Atlantic in 1943, which paved the way for the Allies' later successes in Europe.

Air power, in its infancy in 1914-18, came into its own between the wars and, in 1939-45, the Allies' victory was won as much in the air as at sea. The aircraft carrier succeeded the battleship as the capital ship and, in the great campaign against Japan in the Pacific and Indian Oceans, sea and air power reached an unprecedented degree of sophistication. Both sides were able to strike each others' forces at distances of many miles, and without actually seeing their opponents' ships.

Nonetheless, as throughout history, the war still had to be won on land by armies. So, combined operations were a vital feature of both world wars. That they can be difficult and dangerous was proved by the costly failure of the Gallipoli campaign in

	1900	1910	1920	1930	1940
Society & Technology	Wright brothers fly Elgar	Model T Ford Scott's Antarctic Expedition	Women's vote	BBC	Wall Street Crash Talking pictures	Picasso's *Guernica* Whittle's jet engine	Olivier's *Henry V* ITMA
War & Politics	Queen Victoria dies Entente Cordiale	Balkan conflicts World War I	Russian Revolution	General Strike Mussolini	Hitler	World War II Battle of Britain	Pearl Harbour Hiroshim
Royal Navy	First submarine	Jutland German fleet scuttled at Scapa Flow	WRNS	First aircraft carrier	Radar	Dunkirk Battle of the Atlantic	D-Day
Portsmouth Dockyard	Dreadnought fleet built	HMS *Queen Elizabeth* first oil-fired battleship	**HMS *Victory* restoration**		Construction of cruisers	Air raid damage 25,000 dockyard workers

Carrier force in the Pacific in 1945 by D Cobb

A CORRECTLY DRESSED RATING

- cap on straight
- cap ribbon above ridge of cap
- collar dark blue
- lanyard knot above vee of silk
- centre of badges midway between point of shoulder and elbow
- bight of silk 1-2 in.
- belt to be adjusted to fit neatly around waist, —
- — brass slides close up to buckles
- boots laced over-and-over, not criss-cross

- bow over left ear
- centre of lettering over the nose
- medal ribbons 4½ in. from point of shoulder
- base of rate badge in line with point of G.C. badge
- bow of tapes 3-4 in. across, with ends 5-7 in. long, trimmed swallow-tail, tucked into waist-belt

Class II uniform (Dri...

WOMEN'S ROYAL NAV...

JOIN THE Wrens

AND FREE A MAN FOR THE FLEET

1915-16 and the Walcheren landings in 1944. But, in World War II, there were successful amphibious operations all over the world - the most famousbeing the sea-borne D-Day invasion of Europe in June 1944. The work of the fleet in transporting and landing the troops and supplies, and in defending their lines of communication, was decisive.

Changes in social conditions kept pace with technological change. An innovation was the introduction of women into the Navy in 1917 and again in 1939 - the 'Wrens'. But all aspects of life afloat changed dramatically and, by 1945, the typical sailor was a highly-trained specialist, working complicated and sensitive machinery in ships that would have been beyond the understanding of his predecessors. The age of modern, electronic and computer-controlled warfare had dawned.

M33 is one of only two British warships to survive from World War I. Built in 1915, the 53m (177ft) monitor is a floating gun platform designed to bombard coastal positions from the sea. She saw action at Gallipoli, and later was used to help the White Russians in the White Sea in 1919. Owned by Hampshire County Council Museums Service, she is shown undergoing restoration in No 1 Dry Dock.

Start of an era…building
HMS Dreadnought

End of an era…
the Royal Navy's
last battleship,
HMS Vanguard, runs
aground in
Old Portsmouth while
being towed to the scrap
yard in 1960

Until March 2007 visit the special exhibition at the Royal Naval Museum on HMS *Dreadnought*.

BUILDING BATTLESHIPS & SERVICING THE FLEET

The 20th century had hardly dawned when Portsmouth Royal Dockyard built the epoch-making battleship HMS *Dreadnought* in the astonishing time of 366 days from laying the first keel plate to steaming out of the harbour for trials.

To maintain naval supremacy, Britain constructed a fleet of 'Dreadnoughts'. Whereas *Warrior* had to be built by a private yard because the Royal Yards had neither the skills nor capacity to cope, by the early 20th century Portsmouth Royal Dockyard could build battleships cheaper and more quickly than any other shipyard in the world. Almost one a year came down the slipway. The last was the *Royal Sovereign* which was launched without ceremony as the dark clouds of war gathered over Europe. The dockyard work force had swelled to 25,000 men and women.

Peace brought a decline in the activity and population of the Dockyard - although old skills were revived to repair HMS *Victory* - only to be stepped up again as the threat from Nazi Germany increased in the late 1930s.

World War II brought a deadly new hazard - bombing from the air. Few cities in the kingdom suffered more grievously than Portsmouth, with over 65,000 homes damaged or destroyed. The Dockyard was the prime target and was severely battered. It became too dangerous to repair large warships in dry dock, where they were very vulnerable, and for the first time the yard lost the prestige of being a base for capital ships. However, smaller ships queued for attention. During the war, Portsmouth dry-docked 2,548 warships and repaired thousands more. Operation Overlord, the D-Day invasion in June 1944, saw the Dockyard once more bursting with ships and materials.

The post-war years brought a decline in Imperial commitments and, in consequence, a reduction in the fleet. Although the Dockyard was kept busy fitting ships for minor wars and modernising the fleet to meet the new nuclear and missile age, its role was slowly changing. On 1 October 1984, the Royal Dockyard at Portsmouth was renamed the Fleet Maintenance and Repair Organisation.

DOCKYARD APPRENTICE

The Dockyard Apprentice Exhibition tells the story of Dockyard life in 1911, the time when the great Dreadnought battleships were being constructed in Portsmouth. Visitors clock-in as the apprentices used to do and, with the help of many interactive exhibits, learn about the skills and crafts which built and maintained the formidable British fleet.

When the Falklands War broke out in 1982, a huge task force was assembled in Portsmouth. The Dockyard worked around the clock, loading thousands of tonnes of stores, fuel and ammunition, fitting helicopter pads and guns to merchant ships - all watched by millions on TV. An emotional welcome greeted the return of the fleet.

THE MODERN NAVY AND PORTSMOUTH

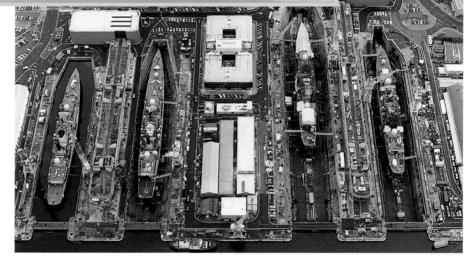

Portsmouth is as much a centre of naval activity as ever, but technology marches on and the ships in harbour belong to a new era - the age of electronics.

Nelson bemoaned his lack of frigates to look for the enemy, and only 90 years ago Jellicoe needed squadrons of cruisers and destroyers to scout for him. Today, one ship fitted with radar can 'see' an area of 2,000 sq miles, as great as that covered by both fleets at Jutland. A modern frigate has only a single 4.5in gun, but in a given time it can deliver a greater weight of shells than the whole broadside of a World War II cruiser.

Warships are not the only grey ships seen in harbour - there are also the tankers and store ships of the 'other' Navy, the Royal Fleet Auxiliary. In the Napoleonic War, the Channel Squadron was able to keep watch off

After 800 years, the fleet is still maintained in Portsmouth

Brest for months on end through the efforts of little hovellers and hoys run by the Navy's Victualling and Stores department. They brought out water, firewood, provisions; everything needed to keep the fleet at sea. Today, the RFA fulfils the same role, but on all seven seas.

Many other craft, operated by the Royal Maritime Auxiliary Service, support the grey ships.

In training establishments all around Portsmouth, young sailors learn their trades. Fifty years ago, radar training had to be carried out on ship. Now, computer simulators allow virtually all training to be carried out more cost-effectively ashore.

In the era of Pax Britannica, the Royal Navy acted as the world's policeman. It still performs the same role, but now normally in the service of the United Nations. More recently Portsmouth ships have been involved in combating illegal drug-running in the Caribbean.

And so often, when there is a natural disaster, news broadcasts will speak of HMS so-and-so or RFA such-and-such being the first to arrive, providing communications and the practical skills which are as much the sailor's stock-in-trade today as they have been for centuries.

The crew stands to attention as HMS Lancaster leaves port.

Much of the Royal Navy's surface fleet is based in Portsmouth. Although at any one time many are at sea, you always see some of the following ships on a 'Warships by Water' tour of the Naval Base:

Aircraft carriers

Portsmouth ships:	*Invincible R05, Illustrious R06, Ark Royal R07*
Displacement:	20,000 tonnes (19,600 tons)
Length:	210m (700ft)
Crew:	682 plus 366 Fleet Air Arm
Armament:	Sea Dart missile system, Phalanx or Goalkeeper gun systems, Sea Harrier fighter/attack aircraft, antisubmarine helicopters
Main purpose:	Forward air base, fleet command and communications

Type 42 Destroyers

Portsmouth ships:	*Exeter D89, Southampton D90, Nottingham D91, Liverpool D92, Manchester D95, Gloucester D96, Edinburgh D97, York D98*
Named after:	Cities
Displacement:	D86 - D92 3,560 tonnes (3,490 tons)
	D95 - D98 3,880 tonnes (3,800 tons)
Length:	D86-D92 - 125m (417ft) D95-D98 - 139m (463ft)
Crew:	266/269
Armament:	114mm gun, Sea Dart missile system, Phalanx gun system, antisubmarine torpedo tubes, close-range guns, Lynx helicopter
Main purpose:	Defence of the fleet against air attack

Type 23 Frigates

Portsmouth ships:	*Lancaster F229, Iron Duke F234, Westminster F237, Richmond F239, Kent F78, St Albans F83*
Named after:	Dukes
Displacement:	3,500 tonnes (3,430 tons)
Length:	133m (444ft)
Crew:	173
Armament:	114mm gun, Harpoon missile system, vertical launch Seawolf missile system, antisubmarine torpedo tubes, close range guns, Lynx helicopter
Main purpose:	General purpose

Hunt Class Mine Warfare Ships

Portsmouth ships:	*Ledbury M30, Cattistock M31, Middleton M34, Chiddingfold M37, Hurworth M39, Brocklesby M33, Quorn M41*
Named after:	Fox hunts
Displacement:	865 tonnes (848 tons)
Length:	57m (190ft)
Crew:	42
Armament:	30mm close-range gun, remote control mine disposal system featuring mini-submarine
Main purpose:	Clearing all types of mines

Offshore Patrol Vessels

Identification:	Castle Class: *Dumbarton Castle P265*
Main purpose:	Policing the waters around Britain, especially North Sea oilfields

Identification:	River Class: *Tyne P281, Severn P282, Mersey P283*
Named after:	Navigable British rivers
Length:	20.8m (68.2ft)
Displacement:	49 tonnes full load
Crew:	11
Armament:	1 x 20mm cannon can be fitted; 2 x 7.62 MGs
Main purpose:	Fishery protection

Others

Antarctic ice patrol ship *Endurance A176*

Royal Fleet Auxiliaries (not Portsmouth based): Fort class store ships (e.g. RFA *Fort Victoria*), Leaf class oilers (e.g. RFA *Brambleleaf*), repair ship RFA *Diligence*, aviation support ship RFA *Argus*

Royal Maritime Auxiliary Service (black hulls and buff superstructures): tugs, fleet tenders (carry stores and equipment) and specialist craft carrying fuel and ammunition

Action Stations occupies the ground and first floors of Boathouse No 6, a former Naval boathouse constructed in the 1840s and one of the first examples of a brick building erected around an internal metal frame. In Victorian times this was revolutionary building practice at the cutting edge of technology. The massive cast iron beams inscribed with their maximum load-bearing capacity supported the many ships' wooden boats that were built and repaired here by skilled dockyard craftsmen.

During World War 2 a direct hit by enemy bombing destroyed the east end of the building at first and second floor level. The gaping void was hastily sealed over by a temporary screen of corrugated iron which remained until the boathouse was declared surplus to Navy requirements in the late 1970s, and then eventually became part of the Historic Dockyard estate in 1986.

When design development commenced on Action Stations in 1996 the bomb-damaged rear part of the building gave architects MacCormac Jamieson Prichard the perfect opportunity to insert the elegant futuristic cinema and, along with its new circular glass stair tower, Boathouse 6 once again became an example of exciting, innovative building technology.

As the Historic Dockyard has grown in popularity with visitors so has interest in the modern Navy, its ships and crews. Nowadays the Royal Navy is less involved in defending Britain from her enemies and more concerned with peace-keeping around the world, humanitarian aid in war zones and natural disasters, and geographical research and surveying. But it is still a highly efficient war machine waiting to spring into action, and its people are among the best-trained and most intensively skilled specialists in the world.

Portsmouth is Britain's premier Naval base. The Defence Review of the early 1980s closed several Naval bases around the country, including Chatham, but Portsmouth has remained operational and is still going strong after more than 500 years. The Historic Dockyard occupies the south-west corner of the Naval Base and is the only part of the base that is open to the public all year round.

The history of the Royal Navy is well told by the three great warships, *Mary Rose*, HMS *Victory* and HMS *Warrior* 1860, and by the Royal Naval Museum

displays which link them together through the centuries. But there is also a great story to be told about the modern Royal Navy of today, which visitors to the Historic Dockyard can see going about its daily business. All around are the sights and sounds of the senior service, the hustle and bustle of a working Naval Base and a thriving collection of docks, workshops, factories and offices, all intent upon servicing the modern fleet. It is this unique dimension that gives the Historic Dockyard its vibrant atmosphere.

In tribute to the Navy of the 21st century, Action Stations aims to bring visitors a real taste of life at sea on one of the most modern warships, the Type 23 frigate. Housed in a huge converted Victorian boathouse, Action Stations invites you to feel the excitement and danger of the Navy in action in a modern-day terrorist scenario, and to take part in a completely interactive experience designed to show whether you measure up to the legendary skill and strength of the Royal Navy and the Royal Marines.

A 25-minute large-format film, *Command Approved* (PG), shows the Royal Navy and Royal Marines at their best, successfully handling a potential disaster involving gold bullion theft, piracy, hostage-taking and a breathtaking exchange of missiles.

A large part of the action was filmed on location on the island of Eleuthera in the Bahamas where two Type 23 frigates, HMS *Marlborough* and HMS *Montrose*, played the role of the fictional HMS *Monarch*. While the main characters were all British actors, extras were recruited from nearby Miami and from the two ships' crews. Filming was completed at Pinewood Studios, home to many a James Bond set, and at the Royal Navy's damage control training school at HMS *Excellent*, Whale Island. The result is a fabulous fast-action drama.

Visitors can also try their own hand at many of the skills seen deployed by naval personnel in *Command Approved*, and can assess their physical fitness against that of the Royal Marines. Specially formulated aptitude tests will let you know if you're Royal Navy material, and for that final thrill take a ride in the 19-seat, six-axis simulator pod.

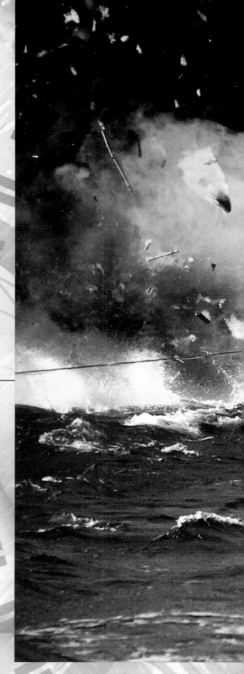

Thrilling scene from *Command Approved*

"COMMAND APPROVED"

ROLL	SCENE	TAKE
B2	38	3

SC99

Director G. MOORE

Camera A. WRIGHT

Date 13/3

MOS DA

Hi tech 275 seat cinema in ACTION STATIONS

INTERACTION GALLERY

Enter the world of marine technology in this captivating gallery, designed to spark the imagination of all members of the family. Twenty-seven exciting educational activities bring you an astronaut's view of the world, the science behind propulsion, state of the art satellite communications, making waves with radio, and building a Type 45 destroyer. See how the moon affects the tides, race a speed boat against a submarine and then sink a submarine by sonar.

Visitors will also discover the amazing Magic Planet which can show moving global climate and temperature patterns around the Earth – and then mysteriously transform itself into any of the other planets in our solar system.

M

A Millennium Commission
Lottery Project

Action Stations is part of the Renaissance of Portsmouth Harbour Millennium Scheme which was 50% funded by the Millennium Commission as one of its Landmark Lottery Projects. In 2005 the attraction received a further contribution from the Commission's ReDiscover Fund towards the InterAction marine technology gallery which opened in February 2006.

FIRE

Published by Portsmouth Historic Dockyard
Visitor Centre
Victory Gate
HM Naval Base
Portsmouth
Hampshire PO1 3LJ

24 hour recorded information line: 023 9286 1512
Administration: 023 9283 9766
Educational and Group Bookings: 023 9283 9766
Marketing and PR: 023 9289 4550
Fax: 023 9283 8228
Visitor Centre: 023 9272 8060
email: enquiries@historicdockyard.co.uk
www.historicdockyard.co.uk

The partners in Portsmouth Historic Dockyard are:
Mary Rose Trust
Portsmouth Naval Base Property Trust
Royal Naval Museum
Warrior Preservation Trust Ltd
HMS Victory

Photographs:
Members of Flagship Portsmouth Trust except:
Colin Thornley (p2); Royal Navy Fleet Photographic Unit
(p3, p43, p44, p47);©Crown Copyright/MOD (p28, p38,
p40, p47); Brian Patterson (p7, p17); Jon Adams (p11);
HBG Special Projects Ltd (p12); Peter Langdown (p12, p45,
p46, p47); Francis Smitheman (p14, p20); Joe Low (p16,);
Science Museum/Science & Society Picture Library (p26);
Imperial War Museum (p35); HCC Museums Service (p37);
Portsmouth Publishing and Printing Ltd (p38); Christopher
Dobbs (p39); Royal Dockyard Historical Trust (p39);
John Dorkings (p48)
Mary Rose contemporary illustration (p10) reproduced by
kind permission of the Master and Fellows of Magdalene
College Cambridge

Design, text pages: © CDA Design, Worthing
Design, cover: Brand New Day, Nottingham
Cutaway drawings and map: Tony Townsend

ISBN 0-9531084-0-6